To Me With Love

Looking Beyond the Pain of the Past to Find Self-Acceptance

Tambre Ross

TO ME WITH LOVE: LOOKING BEYOND THE PAIN OF THE PAST TO FIND SELF-ACCEPTANCE

1405 SW 6th Avenue • Ocala, Florida 34471 • Phone 352-622-1825 • Fax 352-622-1875
Website: www.atlantic-pub.com • Email: sales@atlantic-pub.com
SAN Number: 268-1250

Library of Congress Cataloging-in-Publication number: 2019051144

Ebook ISBN: 9781620237052

Printed in the United States

INTERIOR LAYOUT AND JACKET DESIGN: Nicole Sturk

Over the years, we have adopted a number of dogs from rescues and shelters. First there was Bear and after he passed, Ginger and Scout. Now, we have Kira, another rescue. They have brought immense joy and love not just into our lives, but into the lives of all who met them.

We want you to know a portion of the profits of this book will be donated in Bear, Ginger and Scout's memory to local animal shelters, parks, conservation organizations, and other individuals and nonprofit organizations in need of assistance.

– Douglas & Sherri Brown,
President & Vice-President of Atlantic Publishing

Dedication

This book is dedicated to the following people.

First and foremost to Mary Peeler for believing in me and seeing the light that shined so brightly and for helping me find my true self! To my children—Sean, Jessica, and Kyle— for being my inspiration, my strength, and my never-ending pillar of salvation that drove me to be a better person and to seek true salvation. To my husband, Josh, for not having me committed and standing by my side through all things even when the worst was often hard for both of us to bear. We came through it together with our light shining even brighter. To my clients who have blessed me with the opportunity to be a part of their journey and story of healing. I thank you, and I look forward to many more years of fruitful endeavors.

I am who I am, and I am who I need to be through the grace of God and the love of those who love me. Blessings to all!

Table of Contents

Preface

Someone once told me that to be a great writer you must write what you know and write from your heart. To accomplish this, you must search deep into the depths of your soul. Sometimes the search is painful as you find all the unanswered questions that have somehow wounded your spirit. Then, you must consider if the wounds are healed enough to be dredged up so that you may create a piece that is both passionate and humorous in its own right.

Many of us have skeletons we've hidden behind closed doors, but to seek them out can be healing and be the root of a good story. I have pondered these truths for countless days and nights, considering my own hidden skeletons, and I have come to the conclusion that my secrets are scars, marking my path through life.

I have earned many of these scars, but some have been ruthlessly placed upon me through no fault of my own. There are even a few that, no matter how much thought I put into it,

I can find no explanation for their presence. With each scar that is embedded into our spirit, there comes a story. I have finally found mine, and I am proud to say that I have earned each of my scars through perseverance.

But what about the scars you didn't want or ask for? Those are the ones that make great stories. I have found that with each of my scars, there was a lesson to be learned. The price was often more than I could pay, but I have made peace with each one and have freed myself from the shadows that placed those scars upon me. The skeletons in my closet are now ghosts of distant memories I keep locked deep in the secret chamber of my being. They often try to crawl back in to inflict fear and pain, but I remind myself that I have conquered that battle. But it is for that very reason that they continue to follow.

With the lessons I have learned, I am now free to tell my story and hopefully help others with the scars they carry. I have delved into the depths of my soul and have decided to write exactly what lies within my heart. First I thought of poetry and how my life might resemble some great work from Johann Wolfgang von Goethe or Gandhi, but then I realized that my life seemed more like an Erma Bombeck novel. I am quite fond of her work and carry one of her quotes with me wherever I go: "When I stand before God at the end of my life, I would hope that I would not have a single bit of talent left, and could say, 'I used everything you gave me'." This simple quote lies at the heart of my strength. I have persevered through all that is good and bad, standing tall and proud, knowing that my guardian angel must look far worse than I do. We have fought a good fight, and it had purpose.

Chapter One

"Dear Santa, I want a little brother for Christmas, a fur coat for Mommy, and some tools for my daddy." I wrote this exact list to Santa Claus when I was 5 years old. I remember it as if it were yesterday. One evening, my mother read an old story to me titled *Yes, Virginia, There is a Santa Claus*. The story had me so intrigued that I wrote my request and sealed the letter, trusting my mother to send it to the North Pole. I lay in bed that night, hoping and praying for all that I had requested.

A sudden thought came to mind as I tried to drift off to sleep. How on Earth was Santa going to get my baby brother down the chimney? He couldn't put him in his red bag of gifts, he might suffocate! This thought concerned me until I realized it made much more sense for Santa to just gift wrap him, place a big, pretty bow on the box, and have him delivered to the house through overnight delivery. Perfect! Off to sleep I went.

That Christmas, I did not get my little brother, nor did my mother get her fur coat. My father, however, did get some very nice tools. It was a nice Christmas all in all, but something was still missing. Do not get me wrong, I never went without when it came to gifts. My parents always tried to keep me in supply of the most current Barbie or Strawberry Shortcake dolls. What it boiled down to was that I was lonely. Being an only child was difficult. I had no one to talk to and no one to share the blame for my everyday faults. No one, that is, except for my angels.

I was constantly in trouble, and growing up with a mother who had emotional issues was not an easy task. They say mental traits are inherited from our parents, grandparents, and so on. In my case, my mother suffered abuse at the hands of her own mother and later passed the same on to me. The abuse was not limited to physical but emotional, as well. In wishing for a little brother that Christmas, I wanted to make my mother happy and find my savior, so to speak.

As I grew older, I stopped believing in Santa and stopped wishing for anything that might save me or make anyone else happier. But at 13, I was finally blessed with a 10-pound, bright-eyed baby brother. He brought hope to my life, as well as my parents'. For a time at least, things were good— very good, in fact. Though we had our typical setbacks just like any other family, I quickly realized that my little brother was not my savior; I was his, at least for a brief time.

The one thing that never changed, however, was the secret that I continued to keep to myself about my angels—my guardians, my guides, my true friends. They were the ones I could see, speak to, and hear when, for some reason, no one else could. Why was I so different? Why was I so "off"? Growing up Catholic, I was told that under no circumstance was I to partake in such "nonsense". So, I did what any normal teenager would do, I spoke to my grandmother and found out that I wasn't so "off" after all. It was actually a family trait, but we didn't talk about it. And then the big change came—the female change.

By 16, I was eager to leave home. I was doing well in school and had numerous friends. To anyone who didn't know any better, my life looked perfect. But my home life was anything but. My daily routine consisted of waking up, going to school, coming home, and trying to do anything that wouldn't get my mother's attention and send her into a mood swing. My little brother had become the center of her world, which also made him a target.

My eagerness to leave home and to escape the everyday routine led me straight into the arms of *him*. Let's call *him* Lee. My body was far more mature than my mental and emotional age, and I, like anyone that age, lacked a bit of common sense. I was swooning with what I thought was love for Lee. I wanted freedom, a proper family, and someone to love me for who I was. Leaving my brother was one of the many scars left upon my heart.

The first time I left home was not by choice. My mother had smacked my brother with a rolled up magazine because he was tired and a little whiny. I approached her to defend him, but she turned on me and tossed me down a flight of stairs where I landed hard on my back. As I lay there trying to catch my breath, Lee came rushing down the stairs to my aid. My mother screamed profanities and told me to get my things and leave. I did as she wished, glancing back at my brother and wanting desperately to wipe the tears from his eyes.

As Lee and I drove away, I prayed, "Dear God, please watch over him and keep him safe." A few weeks went by, and I moved in with Lee and his mother. My "trip" down the flight of stairs had injured me, and I was not feeling my usual self, so I had to go see my doctor. I was also late. I didn't have the wonderful cramping that made me feel like I could murder someone that came with nature's cleansing of the female body.

My mother and I were once again on speaking terms, and since I was only 16 and on my father's insurance, I needed her to take me to my appointment. The thought never really crossed my mind that I could be pregnant. Surely the fall would have taken care of that. Besides, it just couldn't happen to me. I was young and working a full-time job after completing my GED. I had to leave high school after being bullied and beaten up by a group of angry gang members.

I was starting a new life with a man I loved and embarking on adulthood much earlier than I had expected. I had many hopes and dreams, and I just couldn't be pregnant. So, off to the doctor I went. I provided a urine specimen in the not-so-pleasant cup the nurse had given me, feeling completely disgusted at the act. Then I gave a tube of blood, which made my stomach lurch and protest my breakfast. Nearly four hours later, the phone rang. I heard my mother answer it and say, "Really? Uh huh… Okay, thank you," before hanging up.

My heart was in my throat. She looked at me and said, "Well, the test was positive. You are pregnant." My checkup entailed no discussion about my unfortunate tumble down the stairs, so all of my symptoms were assumed to be due to my newfound condition. I felt completely numb. I went between feeling scared, helpless, and confused in a matter of seconds. I wavered back and forth between fear and happiness.

Okay, I told myself, *I can do this.* I must and will take responsibility for my actions. I had a tiny being growing within me. Who was I kidding? I was a 16-year-old who'd just found out that she was pregnant, and I was scared to death.

All of a sudden, I heard them—the voices of my long lost angels. *Oh, how I have missed you!* I heard a loud buzzing in my left ear and a chorus choir started to sing the most beautiful angelic music I had ever heard. Then, I heard the softest of voices whisper, "You are not alone, and you're never alone." When I began to cry, my mother naturally thought that it was just a reaction to the news I had received. I couldn't explain the truth to her, so I left it alone, remembering how unwelcome the topic of my angelic visitors were when I was younger. Then it hit me—this was another chance for hope. I could give this child everything I didn't have and everything I wanted. Most of all, I could give it love and understanding.

As I prepared to take my shower that night, I stood in front of the mirror, looking at myself with my hand on my belly. I knew that it would be just a matter of time before my clothes no longer fit. A tear rolled down my cheek, then came another, and I wondered how I was going to tell Lee the news. I told myself that there was only one way to do it, and that was to just do it.

After discussing my new "condition" with my mother, we decided to tell Lee and his mother together the next evening. Lee's father had passed away when he was very young, and he was quite close to his mother. The next evening, we all gathered in Lee's mother's living room. We started with some small talk, but eventually the time came for me to spill it. I looked at Lee and began by telling him that I had gone to the doctor yesterday and had some tests done. He asked me how it went, so I continued, saying that I'd also had a pregnancy test done, and it was positive. The room went silent. I felt a lump slowly crawling up my throat, and Lee just stared at me.

His mother was the first one to speak. As tears rolled down her cheeks, she said, "Congratulations."

Lee sat for a moment and then said simply, "Well, I guess that's that."

The discussion lasted no more than about 30 minutes. Lee was often on again, off again about the pregnancy. He had many family members offer to assist and relieve me of my situation. I kindly declined each time, and let them all know that my mind was made up, and I would be fine no matter what Lee decided to do.

And just like that, the journey of my pregnancy began, and I had to move back home. Not only did my body go through changes, but my emotions and outlook on things were changing too. My angels were never far but were often silent for a great deal of the time. I desperately wanted to hear them and see them to help get me through this. I was trying so hard to figure out how to "call" on them at a moment's notice. Why was I not hearing them when I wanted to, and why is it always so random? It wasn't until much, much later that I realized that they were there all along, preparing and strengthening me for what was yet to come. They were building me up and making me stronger, more independent, and more patient.

Chapter Two

I was on my own for most of my pregnancy, and I almost lost my unborn child because of stress. Once again, my angels came to me. As I was lying in my hospital room after being taken to the ER because of overexertion, I heard, "You will have a strong baby boy, and he will leave you for a short time." The words were both consoling and heartbreaking. What did they mean? I would have a strong boy, and he would leave? I was both happy at the thought that I would carry my child full term and that I was having a son, and confused at the thought of him leaving.

The doctor came in and informed me that I was fine but that I needed to take some time to rest. I needed to stay off my feet and try to keep stress off my plate. I wanted to say, 'Hey, doc, stress is my middle name. I'm a single 16-year-old mother, and I'm just trying to make it. I hear angels and can't tell my own mother without fear of being chastised.' But knowing this would surely wind up putting me in the psych ward, I kept my mouth shut and nodded my head. I let my mother take lead and was released to go home.

Lee slowly came around to the idea of being a dad. As the delivery date for our child came closer, he began to get more involved. I had moved back into his mother's home with him, and we developed our own routine. He worked an evening job while I stayed home with his mom. Somehow, things just fell into place. Then the magical evening came when our son was born. My water broke while Lee was at work, leaving his mother to drive me to the hospital. I'll never forget that drive. It felt long and treacherous even though it was only 10 minutes to the hospital. Her soft words were so consoling.

We make it to the hospital in time for delivery and roughly six hours later, a healthy six-pound baby boy was born. I knew the moment that I saw him that he was special with those deep, serious blue-green eyes. And then I remembered the angel's words, "You will have a strong baby boy, and he will leave you for a short time," and I cried. What did the angels mean? How could this precious baby leave me? He will leave when he goes to college or marries. Surely that was what the angels mean.

Time has a way of going by so fast that if you blink, you miss everything. Lee and I got married five months after our son was born. We had two more children, another boy and a girl, both happy and healthy…well, at least healthy. Many things transpired during our marriage that changed us both, and even contributed to the scars left on the souls of our children.

After we got married, I was no longer allowed to associate with my side of the family. I was often called a "witch" due to my talk of angels and newfound ability to "know things". I was often chastised for speaking my mind, telling the truth, and standing up for our children. We moved several times and rarely called a place home for longer than a year. I burrowed into myself, hiding from the outside world. I shut everything and everyone out, even my angels. I became whatever Lee said I was. I was unhealthy, unhappy, broken, and soiled.

Then, one night, everything came to a head, and I had no control. It was Christmas and we were visiting old friends and staying at a hotel for a few days. Lee had had a few drinks and got angry. Nothing I said got through to him. Just outside our hotel room door, he punched me so hard in the face that I fell to the floor. Once I was down, he kicked me in the ribs.

"Get up!" Lee yelled. "Get up, you stupid bitch!"

I was left lying on the floor, breathless and gasping for air. I prayed my youngest son wouldn't walk out at the noise to find his mother cowering on the floor.

That night I stayed in the room adjacent to the one Lee and I were meant to share. I was afraid to have my youngest son to see the bruises that were already starting to form on my face. I didn't find out until the next morning that Lee had left in the middle of the night, leaving me and our son stranded 300 miles from home.

The morning after the dispute left little and much for my son's little mind to process. "Mom, don't you think it's time to move?" my 8-year-old son said.

"Yes—yes I do, son," were the only words I managed to say. My lip was swollen and every part of me hurt.

My mind was a fog. The day went by as a blur with my son at my side as I held ice packs to my face and ribs. My friend tried to comfort me with friendly, sarcastic humor as the day turned to night. After a phone call home, I knew I was alone. My daughter was forced to become an adult overnight as she, with the help of her friend, rescued her stranded mother and brother. Then, all that was left was to figure out the rest of our lives. That was the real mystery, indeed. My heart ached.

Lee was consumed by the evils of men and money. He wanted things that I could not provide. At some point there was a shift, and we just no longer were able to meet in the middle. His verbal and physical abuse took a toll on me, and I had finally had enough. The chains were broken; I was released. And so, my journey to find the real me and who I really was finally started.

I didn't realize at the time that this was the very situation that my angels had been preparing me for. Two years earlier, I had put myself through nursing school while working in a pediatric clinic in the evening. I would come home and see to the needs of my children. Once they were down for the evening, I would stay up all night to do my homework, try to get at least four hours of sleep, and then do it all over again.

Where was Lee during all of this, you ask? He was usually playing video games or in bed. When it came to work around the house, he was often nowhere to be found, and with the kids, he was more like a child himself than a disciplinarian.

Thankfully, putting myself through school had paid off, allowing me to find decent employment that provided a reasonable income. I was able to stash away some of that income for emergencies unbeknownst to Lee, who was not very good at managing money. On several occasions, Lee took the kids' allowance to spend on himself. I never had any regret about stashing some extra money, and it obviously came in handy. This was a big emergency, and I was glad I had prepared for it.

My rescuers—my daughter and her boyfriend—never said a word as we made our way back home. They didn't have to. I could see it in their eyes and feel it in my soul. She, too, felt betrayed and confused over what had happened and what would soon happen between her parents. She had felt the shift between her parents long ago and had even discussed it with me just before the trip her father and I took that Christmas. I felt ashamed, broken, and rejected because of what had happened, but I also felt freedom attempting to crawl out.

Freedom, fear, and excitement all rolled into one great big ball in my stomach. I could feel the wheels in my head starting to turn as I thought about what in the hell I was going to do once I got back home. As we made our way home, I started to dose off in the back seat when suddenly my left ear began to ring loudly. I opened my eyes and asked my daughter to turn the radio down as I was beginning to get a headache.

She looked at me with a blank stare and said, "The radio's not on, Mom."

"Oh," I replied. But there it was again—the loud, ringing, buzzing sound in my left ear. I laid my head back and closed my eyes, telling myself that it was just the beginnings of a migraine.

Blissful sleep came quickly as the motion of the car rocked my sore broken body into relaxation. That was when I saw her in all her beautiful glory. A woman dressed in a beautiful robe with the most beautiful red hair I had ever seen appeared before my eyes. She was surrounded by a bright angelic glow so blinding that it almost hurt my eyes. As she spoke, I immediately recognized her voice. This woman—this angel—had been sent to me for a reason, I realized. I felt as if I were somewhere else, and as she spoke to me, it was like I could feel the words instead of just hearing them.

Her words were soft, loving, and kind as she took me through what I would call a "brief recap" of recent events and explained some unpleasant things to come. By the time she was finished speaking, I felt no pain, sorrow, or regret, just determination. I knew exactly what I had to do next, and I was going to do it. It was now or never. When I woke up, I looked around, wondering if what I had seen was a dream. Questions were running wild in my head.

Was that my guardian angel? Is she here now? Can I really do this on my own? How do I do this on my own?

I felt determined, but I was also a bit confused. Then my left ear started to ring again and my first thought of how to tackle my current situation came to me. With that I started to make a plan.

Chapter Three

I quickly realized that the ringing in my left ear meant that my angels were trying to communicate with me. Not only were the angels communicating with me, but "others" were beginning to make their presence known to me as well shortly after that trip back home. Looking back now, I know that the others were always there, though the people were different and their methods of communication were not always the same. When I consider my childhood, my angels would often just speak to me. There was no fancy little cosmic explosion, no ears ringing, just speaking.

Children have an innocence that frees them to see and feel without prejudice the light and dark in things that adults can't. I have since realized that I shut things off throughout my adolescence as I became first what my mother wanted me to be and then what Lee wanted me to be. This change stole my innocence and my freedom to see the light. Trauma can bring forth many things, both bad and good—memories of things lost and or forgotten, simple pleasant memories that help to restore the light that has dimmed the soul. It can also bring forth gifts that you never realized you had, not to mention ever fathomed using to help others.

The ringing in my left ear would often signal the start of communication with my angelic friends or my guardian angel, whom I would discover many years later is named Rose. The communication is often words that only I can hear. Sometimes I'll also see images in my head as well. I learned to lean on this, embracing it and trying to tap into it.

It was a struggle, however, transitioning to life as a single parent, with an ability to talk to angels. So I did the only thing I could to put my plan into motion—I moved to a new state to start over.

Now, this is the part that hurt and really tore a hole in my soul, creating another scar. Eighteen years earlier, my angels had told me, "You will have a strong baby boy, and he will leave you for a short time." The time had come for him to leave me and it became all too clear what my guardian angel was referring to. The whole divorce process was difficult for my son. He was 18 and going through his own difficulties in life, learning how to deal with love, heartbreak, and growth.

My son seemed to be angry with the world long before his father and I split up. He rebelled against any type of authority, and I would often catch brief glimpses of his father's habits and aggression within him. I knew I needed to do something, but I didn't know what to do to break the cycle at that time. So, when the divorce took place, my son decided to stay with his father. I became the bad guy in his eyes. I accepted the blame placed on me while also hiding the true nature of the divorce from my son. Meanwhile, his father became his friend and hero. Keep in mind that this was the same man that abandoned me for some time during my pregnancy with this child. The anger within my son grew tenfold and I could no longer reach him. The physical abuse I once suffered at the hands of his father had affected my son and scarred his soul and memories. It got to the point that he lashed out one day to recreate the pain he felt inside upon me.

Before I continue, I must first tell you about an event that took place upon my return home from that horrible trip that set everything into motion. Lee attempted suicide by overdosing on pills and alcohol before wandering around in freezing temperatures with limited clothing on, passing out in a field, and getting frostbite that would later result in the amputation of the toes on both feet. When they found Lee the next morning, the sheriff's office called my 16-year-old daughter, who, in turn, called me. Why they reached out to her first instead of me is still a mystery. That phone call traumatized her and required a great deal of healing.

Even with everything Lee and I had been through on that trip, I went to the hospital to see him. When I arrived, however, Lee immediately began to scream obscenities at me, accusing me of trying to kill him. It broke my heart to see him in that condition. I even started to blame myself. I told myself that this was my fault... if only I had been there... Then my left ear started to ring. I shut it off and ignored it, leaving the hospital.

Lee and my son had moved in with Lee's mother, so, naturally, the two became one and the fight was on. He did everything he could to discredit me, even using our son. One cold morning in early January 2009, my son and his then-girlfriend came by to pick up a few of his belongings. I knew immediately that his father had put him up to the confrontational visit. My son wasn't happy with what I was allowing him to take, and when he realized that I was aware he was really there to spy for his father, he became angry and knocked me to the ground. The whole scene was like something you would see in a mosh pit at a rock concert, but there was no dancing—just a great deal of screaming and pushing.

I remember looking up into my son's eyes as he was about to slam my head into the wall of rocks behind me and thinking, *I love you and I forgive you.* Just then, my daughter's boyfriend at the time grabbed him, pulling him off of me with super-human strength. With all the commotion, the neighbors came outside. The police were called, and my son left to go back home. My youngest son, with no coat on in the snow and tears streaming down his face, stood watching the display. Not only did my youngest son have memories and scars from his father's rage, but now he had a few more from his brother.

I had been planning on moving out of state, but the incident with my oldest son sped up the entire process. A trip to court for an emergency order to leave the state with two minor children was not easy to obtain without the father's consent. However, an advocate from the local battered women's association accompanied me with photos she'd taken of my bruises to show the judge, and the order was granted immediately.

After the scuffle with my oldest son, my home was broken into and anything of any value was stolen, including my grandmother's ring, which I held close to my heart, and my home was left in complete disarray. I was ready to leave, ready to start over, and ready for the nightmare to end. I rented a U-Haul and loaded it up with what few possessions I had left. I was angry—angry at God and angry at myself. I just wanted to get away from everything and everyone.

I found a cute little house to rent in Oklahoma, and for the first time I felt free. But freedom came at a price. My daughter and youngest son stayed with my parents, with whom I'd recently reconnected. It had been at least five years since my last phone call to them, and even that was done in secret. I wanted my children to have an easy transition to the new house since they had already been through such a great ordeal. I wanted to set up the house before they came so they'd arrive to a real home.

The nights were long, and I was on my own. I would often wake up and walk through each room, ensuring that every window and door was locked. Nightmares came often, and I struggled with self-doubt and blame daily. I was officially alone. I would sit in my room at night and listen for the ringing in my ear—nothing. I would ask why all this craziness had to happen, but there were never any answers. Eventually I finished the house, and all but one of my kids came home to me.

My anger eventually subsided but developed into something else—something sadder and almost untouchable. I wanted to know exactly why I had received a warning about my son 18 years earlier if I couldn't stop it or change it. Why did my son leave? Why did the divorce happen? Why did this feel like my fault?

I sought counseling for a while as part of the court order for co-parenting and followed through with everything I was supposed to do. I made the monthly trips to Kansas with the two kids to drop them off with their father, but I cried all the way home afterwards. Lee would never drive halfway as the court had ordered, but I no longer had the energy to fight him. As long as the kids wanted to see their father, I would make the full drive.

But after a while, they no longer had the desire to see him. Apparently, the only thing Lee would talk about during the visits was how terrible I was and about all the bad things I had ever done. The environment became too uncomfortable for them, and they no longer wanted to go, so the driving stopped.

Since Lee didn't comply with the court orders and never paid the kids' health insurance or the $100 a month child support per child, I decided that I didn't need to continue driving the kids over 300 miles each way once a month. Lee never fought me on it, and the kids didn't hear from him again for about seven years. There were no birthday or holiday cards and no phone calls—just silence. At one point, I did receive a check for backlogged child support, but it only accounted for a year's worth. I eventually applied for state medical insurance for the kids since I couldn't afford any other type on my salary.

I would send a weekly text message to my oldest son—desperately trying to let him know that I loved him—and a birthday card and gift card every year, but I never received a response. I reached out through social media just to check on him, but it was no use. The pain I felt was unbearable. My heart hurt; there was a part of me that was out there somewhere, and I had no idea if he was safe. Did he really hate me that much? He finally responded one day through social media to tell me as such that he did in fact hate me and that I needed to "just move on and leave him alone."

I backed off a bit, but I couldn't help myself completely. Instead of weekly text messages, I sent monthly ones. I continued to spiral and eventually hit rock bottom. I'd finally lost all hope of ever hearing from him again. I tried to put myself back together again because I knew I had to set an example of strength in independence as a single mother. I had not been appropriately setting that example, and I knew it. My daughter had gone away at school by this time, and my youngest son was beginning to spiral into his own mental nightmare from everything, and I had to do something. *God help me please!*

I began to pray and listen for my angels again. I even started to date. I was able to gain better employment with better pay. I was able to better support my kids, and for the first time in a long time, I felt good about myself, about life, and about the future.

One afternoon in July, I met JR through my job. I won't lie, at first I thought that he was a bit annoying, but something about JR made me feel like I could be myself. I was discovering exactly who I was, slowly but surely.

After a great deal of time had passed, JR and I developed a great friendship and eventually fell in love. JR helped the kids and me heal in ways that I never thought would be possible, and the pain slowly slipped away. It was what I would call out of reach at least for the time being. We later married and JR adopted my two younger kids with the agreement from Lee that we would not bother him for any past-due child support. JR had agreed to all of Lee's few requests, and the adoption went through without any issues.

Chapter Four

My life was definitely in a better place and the kids were doing much better all in all. Don't get me wrong, there were plenty of ups and downs, struggles and thoughts of *Shit, what now?* but something was still missing. Then, one night as I lay in bed, my left ear began to ring and I began to hear beautiful angelic music.

Yes! They're back! I sat straight up in bed and looked around, but *poof*—it was gone. *Shit! Did I imagine that?* Surely not, I know what I heard so I lay back down. I waited for what seemed like an hour before I heard it again. This time I lay still with my eyes closed and just listened. The music played softly, coming from nowhere but everywhere, and as I lay there listening, I drifted off to sleep.

"There you are," she said. "I've been waiting for you."

"It's you!" I said. The only question I could think to ask in that very moment was "Why?"

I received one simple response: "You're not ready."

I asked again. I mean let's face it, 'why' covers a whole lot of ground. I'm human after all, and my life has been like one great big wrecking ball of chaos.

The beautiful, red-headed angel informed me that I still had a great deal of things to do, and I needed to learn my purpose. She said that each and every obstacle I had been through was meant to prepare me for greater things, and in time that purpose would release all the pain I harbored and I'd go on to show others how to do the same.

"It's not yet time to know the 'why' but the 'how.' She gave me direction, and with that, I woke up, feeling refreshed and ready for the day.

I knew my visitor had been sent for a reason. This time I wanted answers—answers to my past, my present, and about why all these things were happening to me. My life was in a better place, the kids were doing great, and I was not exactly sure what was going on with me. I hadn't informed JR of my "gifts" and was actually afraid of what he might think, so I kept much of that to myself. Besides, it had been some time since I'd had a "visitor". But now I had a hunger to know more, and the word 'spirituality' popped into my head like a song.

I could no longer consult with my grandmother for advice since she had since passed away, but, oh, how I wanted and needed her guidance. I always knew she was with me, though, because in my many times of need I could actually smell the perfume she would always wear—Timeless—and often feel her touch my cheek.

So, this was up to me to figure out, and I made the decision to go back to school. I put the past behind me as much as I could and thought, what better to major in than psychology? Being a nurse for 13 years had been a beautiful adventure—one that had helped to get me through a great deal of things while my kids and I transitioned into our new life. I would often see things that I just couldn't quite explain, and having my "gift", I learned how to deal with things in my own way and not make a skeptic of myself. I learned how to "ground" and "channel", but calling on my angels at will was still a challenge.

I would have dreams of things yet to come, and then *boom!* Like a horror movie they would happen. There were still so many things going on within me that I couldn't explain and new things were beginning to happen that I had never experienced before, and I just had no answers. There was only a very small circle of people I could talk to about my problems. So, psychology just seemed like a logical course for me, and so I enrolled in college to pursue my bachelor's degree.

The journey took me on exploration of my own psyche, heart, spirituality, and hidden chambers of pain. It was through this process that I realized that, even with all that I had gone through, I was never alone. I learned about my faith, my trust, and each and every one of my scars. I pulled apart my past and my present and analyzed everything only to realize that I couldn't have changed anything. It is what it is, and was what it was.

That's what brought me to Mary.

One day, an old friend and I were talking about my studies and my conflicted dilemma of spirituality versus psychology that I'd discovered on my path of "finding myself". I was never afraid of my gifts; I was more curious; I needed a better understanding of where they came from and how to use them appropriately, not to mention why they happened at some of the most random times. My friend told me about a woman named Mary Peeler, who's a psychic medium, and how she had been to see her with a group of coworkers.

My friend informed me that she had made an appointment for herself to see Mrs. Peeler, and she invited me to tag along because she could split the visit as a couple's reading. I had never been to see a psychic medium and really didn't know much about them outside of what I'd seen on television or read in books, so I was actually pretty excited and agreed to go. Besides, I was hoping deep down that she might have the answers I needed to put everything to rest.

Prior to our visit with Mary, I kept thinking about all the questions I wanted to ask her; I even made a list. I wanted to know why I heard angel music, why I could hear and speak with those who have passed on, and so many more things. Why was I so different? My list seemed as endless as my energy as it buzzed and grew stronger. It was almost as if the universe knew I was going to see Mary.

On the day of our visit, the front door opened, and we were greeted by a petite older woman and lots of hugs. These hugs were so genuine that they almost knocked me off my feet. This woman didn't even know us, but here she was, hugging us! Once we settled in comfortable chairs and the introductions were concluded, I went completely stone-cold dry-mouthed and forgot every question I had and couldn't bring myself to pull the list out of my purse. I was enveloped in an unseen embrace of love as Mary went straight into the reading.

I was fascinated at the knowledge she had of my friend's issues. *I, too, can do this,* I said to myself. *Is this the same thing I often do?* I wondered. *Where does this come from?* I asked myself.

All of a sudden, Mary turned toward me and asked, "What in the hell are you doing here?"

"Ma'am?" I asked.

Mary then asked, "Who's hearing the angelic music?"

I slowly raised my hand as if I were in elementary school. Feeling embarrassed and a bit foolish, I looked to my friend for help, who in turn gave me an "I told you so" look. I didn't know that while I was asking those questions in my head, Mary had heard all of them and was bouncing the answers back at me telepathically. I was just refusing to hear the "ping".

Mary proceeded to read me and tell me things about my past, my present, and my journey of finding myself. She was blunt, honest, and hit a few nerves about my scars. She spoke about spirit, angels, guidance, and faith. That's when my human eyes closed and my spiritual eyes opened like someone was shining a flashlight in my eyes.

I began to cry, letting out all the pain and horror of my past, letting it all go. I cried so hard that my chest hurt and my eyes were puffy. Feeling a bit embarrassed at my reaction, I apologized to both Mary and my friend who had begun to cry as well. I slowly regained some composure of myself as I felt the weight of the world had been removed from my shoulders and some of those scars had an identity. Mary went on to inform me that it was God's will that I do this work!

"Okay," I whisper in a sob. *Wait, what?*

The session lasted just over an hour, and my heart felt free, my past finally unloaded and the skeletons finally revealed. Scars were revealed, accepted, and accounted for. Who knew that one simple session with a psychic medium could unload and unleash such pain and provide closure? Closure! That's what I had been looking for and needing for so long yet had been unable to find. Yet here was this petite woman with her God-given ability to help give me that peace I needed. The spirits of my grandmother and birth father took turns speaking through this woman to tell me things no one else could possibly know.

"Love," she told me, "is not just an emotion, but an attitude—one that you have displayed with great compassion. Take off your veil and show your true self."

After my session with Mary, I went home, composed myself, and discussed my own abilities with JR. I took some time before, however, to contemplate just how to drop the bomb on him that I could speak with angels and spirits. I knew it could go one of three ways: he would have me committed, he'd divorce me, or he'd accept me. So, after three long years of marriage, I finally told JR about my gifts, and he accepted them with a happy heart.

I completed my degree in psychology and became good friends with Mary, who also became my mentor. Mary encouraged me, taught me self-control, and built me up to be the person I am today spiritually—a gifted psychic medium who is no longer hidden by doubt, shadows, or pain. After all, love, is not just an emotion but an attitude. I have since taken off my veil and am allowing my true self to be seen.

Chapter Five

After my introduction to Mary and my first session with her, a change occurred within me. I started to notice things more keenly. I started to read every book I could get my hands on to learn more about psychic abilities and what it meant to be a medium. I learned how to focus my attention and intent both inwardly and outwardly and learned how to see the goodness in all things. However, I also realized that my abilities made me a target for negativity.

I armed myself with knowledge and empowerment and accepted all these things that were going on within me, even accepting the quest that God had in store for me. With a great deal of guidance from Mary, my spiritual journey slowly but steadily progressed. During my journey, something amazing that Mary and my angels foretold came to fruition.

It was a Saturday evening in June 2015 and it was raining drearily. It was that kind of rain that makes you feel lazy and want nothing more than to curl up on the couch to reflect on things past and present. The phone rang, and when I answered it, my heart went straight to my feet. The voice on the other end of the line was that of my first-born child—my son.

My God, I thought immediately. *It's been years and my prayers have been answered.* Tears slowly fell as I sat frozen, listening as my son simply said, "Hello, Mom, it's me. I have something I need to tell you."

Seven years can feel like 20 when you are separated from the ones you love, especially if it is your child. For a moment, I couldn't speak. The lump in my throat threatening my air supply. I was shaking, and I knew that I had to be careful about my response to not to make him angry. My mind began racing to find the right words that would envoke a positive response.

I replied simply, "I'm glad you called, son. It's been a long time."

We talked for over an hour, and my son let out a great deal of his own pain and emotions over the phone. Being over 300 miles apart, it both hurt and comforted me to finally hear the words: "I'm so sorry, Mom. I was wrong."

But, oh, how I wanted to hold my son in my arms. I learned much about what his life had been like over the past few years—from his ups and downs to the main reason he was calling. Not only was he calling to apologize, but he had met someone special whom he wanted me to meet. He said that I was going to be a grandmother.

A grandmother! Oh, how my angels were dancing!

The call ended after we made arrangements to meet in a few weeks up in Kansas City. I had a newfound hope surging through my spirit. Within an hour's time, life changed for me yet again. I had a grandchild on the way, and my son and I were in the process of repairing our relationship. The next few weeks seemed to drag on as I anxiously prepared for my trip to see my son and his soon-to-be bride.

When the day came to make the trip, a bit of apprehension and panic began to creep into my heart along with a few of those ghosts I mentioned before. I believe JR somehow sensed what I was feeling, because he held my hand throughout the entire six-hour drive.

After my luggage was unloaded and taken up to our hotel room, I spent the next hour pacing the lobby as I waited for my son's arrival. We had decided to meet in the hotel's lobby area because it was a neutral location and he was still living with his father. The lobby had a nice, cozy sitting area in an outdoor garden that was perfect for an intimate meeting. The time we had agreed to meet arrived, and I was a nervous wreck. I kept asking JR if I looked okay. I had been worried about picking the right outfit—I certainly didn't want to be over- or underdressed.

I stopped pacing when I saw his truck pull into the parking—he had described it to me on the phone. My heart skipped a beat and my palms started sweating. I had to tell myself to hold it together.

Sensing my sudden shift, JR squeezed my hand and whispered, "It's okay, babe. This is what you have dreamed about."

My son parked the truck, and I took a deep breath as he opened the door and stepped out. As soon as he saw me, the smile I had seen so often when he was a child spread across his face. He walked towards me with his arms open wide and said, "Hi, Mom," as he wrapped his arms around me. I finally got to hold my son again.

I wept. I just couldn't hold it back; it was the last bit of my brokenness, my heart, my scars, and the ghosts. That which was foretold to me so many long years ago had come true, but was now coming full circle. I gave in to everything—to the moment, to spirit, and to myself. I finally understood.

I didn't have to like the process, but I understood. I knew the "when" that I had asked so many years ago, I had been working on the "how," and I was finally coming full circle to the "why".

When pain leads us down a path away from normal life, we tend to try to find the easiest route back, often inadvertently taking a wrong turn and creating a vicious cycle of pain. We run from one path because it may bring reminders of painful memories that are overwhelming and just too much to bear. But through the fire of pain, we can forge the answers we seek.

JR and I were introduced to my son's fiancée, a cute fireball who was half his height—I immediately knew that my son had met his true match. I could tell that she was someone who would not only care for him but help make his dreams come true, providing him love and compassion while also showing him forgiveness. Yes—forgiveness. Inside this petite woman, a tiny baby boy was growing, and this baby boy would turn my son's world upside down. This baby boy would inherit my gifts. The angels had yet another plan. I smiled as I touched the belly of my soon-to-be daughter-in-law.

We visited for several hours before parting ways with the agreement to be present for the wedding in September. It was a small, beautiful ceremony—one which offered a chance for more healing to take place; not just for myself, but for all three of my children as well. I was so wrapped up in the excitement of having my son back in my life and a grandchild on the way that I completely failed to think about how I was going to have to come face to face with Lee at the wedding.

On the day of the wedding, my emotions were all over the place as JR and I made the long drive to Kansas City from Oklahoma with our daughter and youngest son in tow. They were in the backseat, partaking in jokes and games of I Spy to pass the time. I know in my heart that they, too, were nervous—it had been so many years since either of them had seen or spoken to Lee, and the thought of it likely terrified them a bit.

JR was their pillar of strength, but I, too, had a powerful weapon that I was becoming more accustomed to using—faith. I had grown stronger in my faith and had been working with my spirit friends. I was learning how to protect myself from negativity, ground myself, and even shield others from negative energy. So I did a lot of quiet prayers and meditations during the drive up to Kansas City. To everyone else, it just looked as if I was spacing off out the window.

As we pulled up to the event, I felt his energy. For a moment, the old terror pulled at my heart. I could hear that last time he hit me; I heard the slap, felt the pain, and saw the darkness. I wanted to run. But then my daughter came up and took my hand, saying, "Well, let's do this!"

With that, I pushed the darkness aside, invited the light in, put my shield up, and looked right at Lee. *Oh dear God, he's walking this way. Please don't start anything—not here, not today!* I put on my best face, smiled, and said the only thing my voice allowed: "Hello."

Lee was surprisingly cordial, but I could tell that the past several years had not been kind to him. He looked 20 years older, worn out, and somewhat unhealthy.

The wedding day, however, was a success. It was a beautiful experience in so many ways. As the day progressed, old friends and family members I hadn't seen in ages had approached and engaged in small talk. The awkwardness slowly slipped away, and I knew that my spirit friends were close by. Lee and I even had a moment of reconciliation that was long overdue, and I was finally gifted with the "why" answers I had been waiting years for from him. Another scar, another skeleton, and another memory at last to be tucked away. Though I guess I really was not ready for the answers I received, I still accepted them.

I think it was easier to accept the answers because I had forgiven myself, and I knew within me that things were what they were because they had to be and the harbored emotions were finally banished. I made my choices the same as Lee, and growth happened for both of us. Somehow I felt so different—I felt new, with a strange sort of peace inside of me that I had never felt before. Prior to the end of the evening, my oldest son requested a family photo and, naturally, I couldn't deny him his request. He wanted a photo of himself with his mother and father on his wedding day, and it's a photo I still hold very dear to my heart.

Chapter Six

Six months after the wedding, my beautiful, bright-eyed, bouncing grandson was born, and, as my spirit friends had informed me, I knew immediately that he was special. The whole family, including Lee, was there to welcome this beautiful baby into the world. Lee and I took a trip to the nursery to check in on the newest member of the family. As he and I stood at the nursery window looking in at our grandson, Lee looked at me, took my hand, and said, "At least we did one thing right."

That was the last time I saw Lee alive. Twenty-four days later, he was killed in an auto accident. During the trip to visit my new grandson, I was struggling with the realization that my gifts were changing and increasing in some areas. I had had a very vivid dream about an auto accident just two weeks prior, and I had seen everything and felt everything happening. For some time, I had developed a habit of writing down my "events" and intuitive feelings, and the dream was heart-wrenching. As soon as Lee and I parted that day at the hospital, I knew it was going to be the last time we spoke. And yes, it bothered me.

They say that the life of those who die carry on in those who are left behind. To that I would reply with a simple: "Yes— yes it does." Those who pass on do not want us to grieve for an eternity; they want us to live life in its entirety because our loved ones can see life through our eyes. Life is lived through my children and through their children. The day of our son's wedding, both of us achieved forgiveness once and for all, and peace finally came for Lee.

That dream and the events that took place during the months shortly after taught me just how important it is to never leave anything unsaid, no matter how painful it is to say the words. Life had come full circle for me, and I knew exactly who I was. I knew my purpose in this life, where I needed to be, how I got there, and why.

Conclusion

Many have asked me if there is anything I would have changed about my spiritual journey. In all honesty, there's not. And I mean that with a sincere heart. Let's face it, though I may be tempted to say yes, my spirit says no because without each one of my life lessons and challenges, I would not be where I am today. It is through each one of my challenges, hardships, and emotional embraces that I have come to love myself. It took a great deal of searching to realize that not everything I faced was punishment. It was all due to my actions and choices, and because of that, it taught me how to live.

I cannot place blame on others for my own mishaps, and I cannot dwell on past events. Things in our lives happen at times by chance. Others are a result of our actions and choices, but they should never be reflected upon as punishment. I have locked the skeletons away and embraced my scars, and I know that they do not define me. I am a child of

God with a purpose and a strong desire to embrace life and live it to the fullest.

It has been many years now since my first visit with Mary Peeler, and she has become my mentor, my confidant, and my friend. Shortly after that first visit and the discovery of my true purpose, I was led by my spirit guides and angels to provide a reading for Mary one day while I was driving to work. Naturally I was hesitant and argued with both myself and my spirit friends, informing them that I had no right to "read" for Mary. I mean, seriously—*the* Mary Peeler? She's Oklahoma City's most well known psychic medium. Who was I to read for her? But my spirit friends were insistent, so after I parked my car at work, I began the text that would initiate my professional career as a psychic medium.

Shortly after I sent the text message, Mary called me and invited me to lunch. At our lunch meeting, she confirmed everything I had told her via text. She told me that she had prayed that God and her angels would send someone she could refer her own clients to once she retired. She said that her prayers had been answered. I was without words.

We have been meeting for tuna sandwiches or Panera Bread ever since just to catch up and to engage in normal conversations. Mary assisted me in putting together my own website and walked me through the basics of starting up my small ministry. She eventually retired, referring many of her clients to me. She has blessed me in so many ways, and I enjoy catching up with her when we have our lunch dates. Her clients, too, have been an absolute joy to visit with.

Over these last few years of searching, I had struggled with overcoming my own doubts and fears about who I truly was, as well as overcoming the fear of "coming out", so to speak, with the truth about my spiritual gifts to others. Once I was able to come to terms with my past, my future seemed that much more inviting and hopeful. The fear of rejection and prejudice about my gifts seemed meaningless once I decided to pursue my calling. My spirit friends were always my biggest cheerleaders in helping me to overcome my doubts and fears. They often found a viable—if not so subtle—way to validate things for me.

I wrote this book in the hope that it will touch at least one soul, and if that soul is you, just know that you are never alone and there has been someone there before you. Pain, whether emotional or physical, can be a very significant and spiritual reminder that you are human. If you question long enough and fight hard enough, you can make it through anything. Matthew 7 says, "Ask, and it shall be given you; seek, and ye shall find; knock, and it shall be opened unto you. For every one that asketh receiveth; and he that seeketh findeth; and to him that knocketh it shall be opened."

I am now a proud grandmother of three beautiful grandchildren. Both of my sons and my daughter are doing quite well in their chosen professions and are working on mending their relationships with each other one day at a time. It makes this mom's heart swell every time I get to snap a family photo with all three of them in it. I am so proud of everything the three of them have accomplished even in the midst of the darkest of times. Even though my challenges were often theirs as well and many of my own choices and actions had repercussions that affected those I love so deeply, forgiveness is at the heart and the root of my transformation.

My relationship with my mother has changed for the better over the course of the past few years, as well, and she accepts the things that were not so openly discussed when I was younger. My angels are welcomed and my spirit friends are often asked for guidance. As our relationship healed, I learned that my mother also went through dark times. She fought her demons, came to terms with them, and was left her with her own battle scars.

If I have learned anything, it's that we are all loved unconditionally, we are never alone, forgiveness comes from deep within and is free even though it may be difficult at times, and we are always gifted a second chance. My journey brought challenges, sure, but it also brought change. Like I said earlier, I wouldn't change anything about my journey— would you?